THE CONSTELLATION CYGNUS

MEG THACHER

childsworld.com

Published by The Child's World®
800-599-READ • www.childsworld.com

Photography Credits
Photographs ©: Shutterstock Images, cover (illustration), cover (background), 1 (illustration), 1 (background), 2 (illustration), 2–3 (background), 6 (illustration), 15, 17, 22, 25, 26 (background); E. Slawik/NSF/AURA/M. Zamani/NOIRLab, cover (constellation), 1 (constellation), 2 (constellation), 6 (constellation); Fabio Lamanna/Shutterstock Images, 5; WIYN/KPNO/NSF/AURA/H. Schweiker/NOIRLab, 8; KPNO/NSF/AURA/Adam Block/NOIRLab, 9; Tomas Slovinsky/Shutterstock Images, 11; Aino Kirillova/Shutterstock Images, 13; Lester Graham/Shutterstock Images, 14; Fine Art Images/Heritage Images/Hulton Fine Art Collection/Getty Images, 18; Paolo e Federico Manusardi/Electa/Mondadori Portfolio/Hulton Fine Art Collection/Getty Images, 21; Maria Skrigan/Shutterstock Images, 26 (couple); Ryan Hallock/Flickr, 29; Design elements from Shutterstock Images

ISBN Information
9781503875791 (Reinforced Library Binding)
9781503876217 (Portable Document Format)
9781503876835 (Online Multi-user eBook)
9781503877337 (Electronic Publication)

LCCN 2025938259

Printed in the United States of America

ABOUT THE AUTHOR

Meg Thacher teaches astronomy at Smith College in Massachusetts. She is the author of *Sky Gazing: A Guide to the Moon, Sun, Planets, Stars, Eclipses, and Constellations*. She writes books and articles about science, classical music, and mythology, but mostly astronomy. The Summer Triangle is her favorite asterism because she used to watch it during summer camp.

TABLE OF CONTENTS

CHAPTER ONE

The Constellation Cygnus

When humans first looked at the stars, they saw bright, sparkling lights on a vast black sky. They connected the stars into shapes. These shapes are called constellations. Some constellations are bright. Some are dim. Cygnus (SIG-nuss), the Swan, is bright and easy to find.

Stars are huge balls of gas. Most are hundreds of times larger than Earth. Stars make their own energy, heat, and light. Earth's Sun is a star. Other stars are very far away, so they appear smaller and fainter than Earth's Sun. But many are larger and much brighter.

People throughout history have used the movement of the constellations to keep track of time and the changing seasons.

Stars and constellations rise and set like the Sun does. They seem to move across the sky. Some can be seen all the time. Some can be seen only in certain seasons. Long ago, people told stories about the constellations. These stories helped people remember where the stars were. They helped people track the seasons.

There are 88 official constellations. The constellations recognized today were mostly created by the Mesopotamians, Greeks, and Romans. Most star names come from Arabic texts. But nearly every society has constellations. People around the world made pictures in the sky.

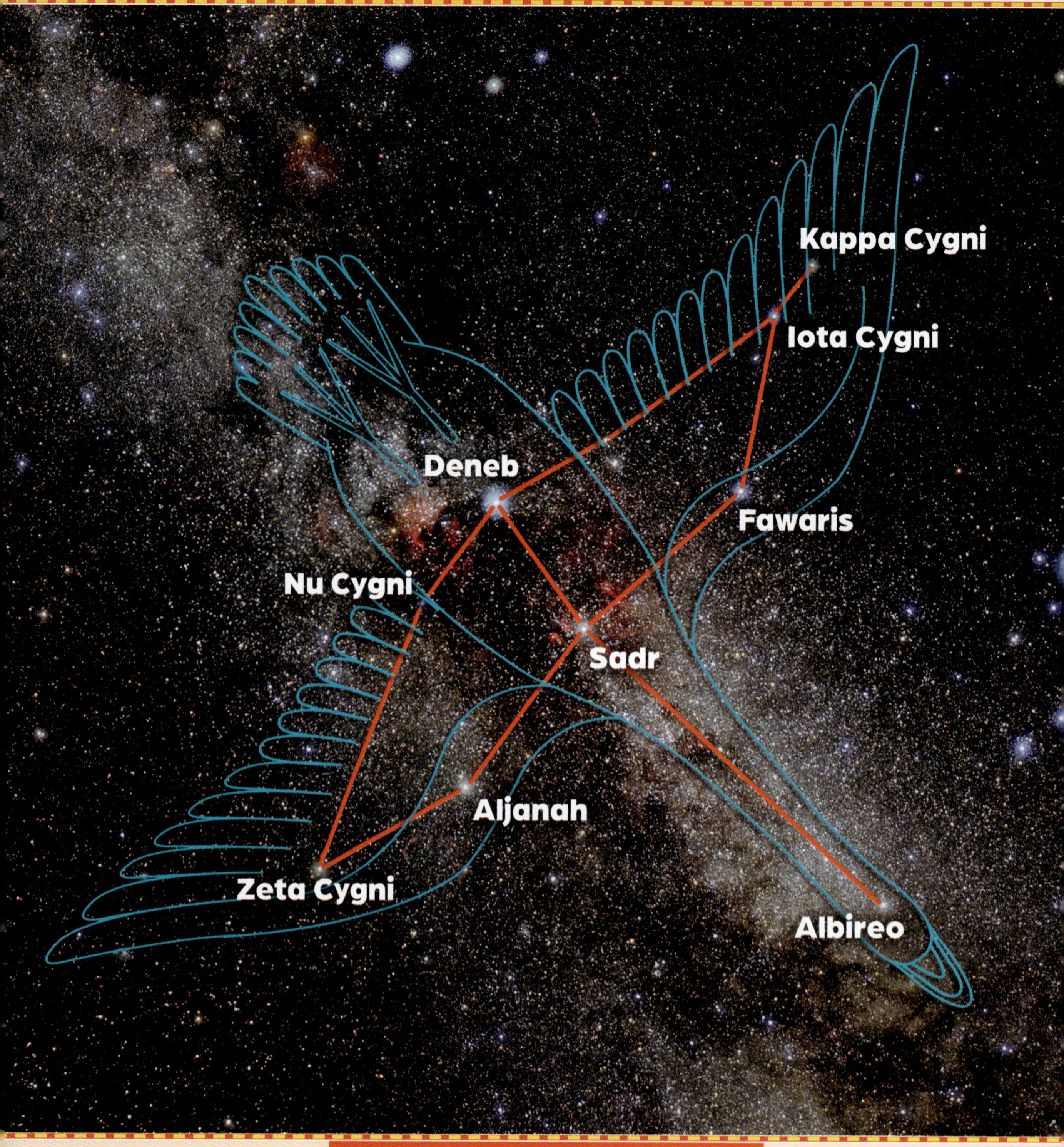

Nine stars make up the Cygnus constellation.

The brightest star in Cygnus is called Deneb (DEH-nehb). It is near the swan's tail. The star Albireo (al-BEER-ee-oh) is the swan's head. It looks like only one star with the naked eye. But Albireo is a double star. Through a telescope, people can see two stars. One star is orange, and one is blue. The blue star is hotter than Earth's Sun. The orange star is cooler.

Cygnus seems to fly along the Milky Way. This is Earth's **galaxy**. The Milky Way stretches across the sky like a starry river. People can see its arms in dark skies. They can use binoculars to see star clusters within this milky band. Star clusters are groups of stars that are packed together.

The sky is divided into sections based on the constellations. There are many star clusters in Cygnus. Messier 39 (M39) is near Deneb. On very dark nights, it is visible with the naked eye. People using binoculars or a small telescope can see about 30 stars. M39 is 800 **light-years** away. The stars in this cluster are younger than the Sun.

Messier 39 is an open cluster. Its stars are not as close together as some star clusters.

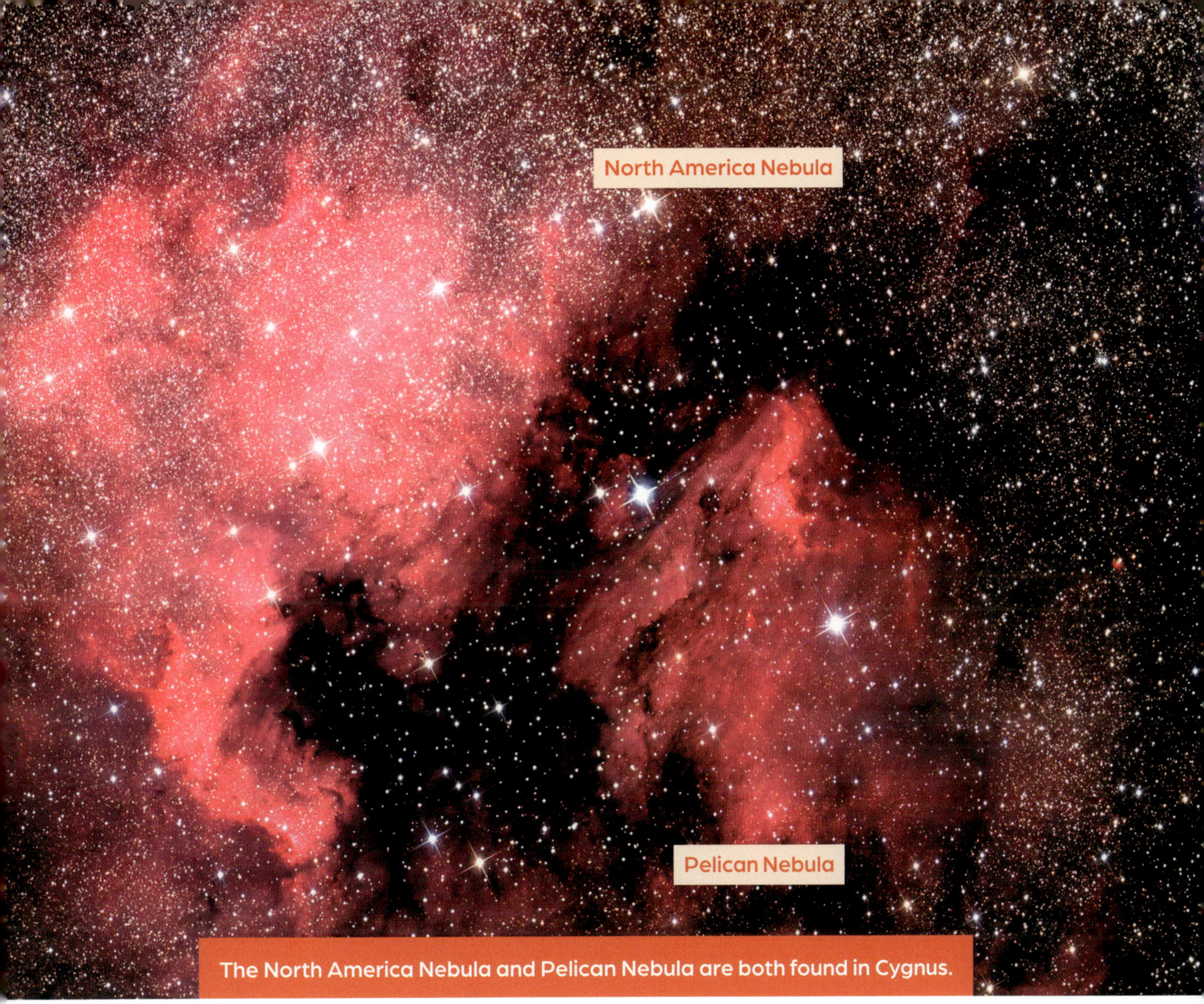

The North America Nebula and Pelican Nebula are both found in Cygnus.

Near M39 is the North America Nebula. A nebula is a cloud of dust and gas in space where stars are born. The North America Nebula is very faint and red. The giant cloud of gas can be seen through binoculars or a small telescope.

In 2009, the Kepler spacecraft was launched into space. Its mission was to find new planets. It discovered more than 2,600 planets **orbiting** stars in Cygnus.

Cygnus is also home to a black hole. Cygnus X-1 is the first black hole ever observed. In 1964, **astronomers** discovered **X-rays** coming from Cygnus X-1. The X-rays are the light from material falling into the black hole.

An asterism is a group of stars that is not an official constellation. Asterisms can be part of a constellation. Or they can be made of several constellations. There are two main asterisms in Cygnus. One is called the Northern Cross. The other is the Summer Triangle. One of the Summer Triangle's points is the bright star Deneb. The two other stars in the triangle are Vega and Altair. Vega is in the constellation Lyra, the Harp. Altair is in Aquila, the Eagle.

BLACK HOLES

When a star much larger than the Sun dies, it can become a black hole. Black holes have a lot of mass in a tiny space. Not even light can escape their gravity. This means black holes are invisible. Astronomers can find them by looking at how they affect other objects.

The Northern Cross asterism is entirely within Cygnus. The Summer Triangle includes stars from two other constellations.
Cygnus
Summer Triangle
Northern Cross
Lyra
Aquila

CHAPTER TWO

The Origin of the Myth

Cygnus is an **ancient** Greek constellation. The ancient Greeks lived in southern Europe beginning around 1200 BC. Their myths are stories of gods and heroes. These myths were first told long ago. They were not written down right away. They changed as they were passed from person to person. The ancient Greeks later wrote plays and poems about the gods and heroes. They made beautiful sculptures and paintings.

Some myths had morals. They told people how to behave. Other myths explained how the universe was created. Still other myths explained events in nature, such as the seasons. Many myths told people how to worship the gods.

The ancient Greeks had many gods. People worshipped these gods to make good things happen or to keep bad things from happening. Each god had a different job and ruled over a different part of life.

Mount Olympus is the tallest mountain in Greece.

The gods lived on Mount Olympus. But sometimes they visited the human world. They helped heroes on their quests. They punished people who behaved badly. Sometimes they fell in love with humans and had children with them.

Most swans have Cygnus in their scientific name, including the trumpeter swan (*Cygnus buccinator*).

Many versions of Greek myths were told. There were more than ten characters in Greek mythology named Cygnus or Cycnus, another way to spell this name. In some stories, Cygnus is the son of Ares, the god of war. In others, he is the son of the King of Liguria. Many versions of the character were turned into a swan.

One of the myths of Cygnus involves Zeus and Apollo. Zeus was the leader of the gods. Apollo was one of his sons. Apollo was the god of many things, including music, poetry, and archery. He also became known as a god of the Sun. Every day, Apollo drove his Sun **chariot** across the sky.

Phaethon (FAY-ih-thun) was the son of Apollo and a human woman. Cygnus was his best friend. Some stories say they were relatives. Phaethon made a big mistake, and Cygnus tried to help him. The gods turned Cygnus into a swan and put him into the sky. He is there to remind people of true friendship.

In some stories, Phaethon is the son of Helios. Helios was the original Sun god. Over time, more people associated Apollo with the Sun.

CHAPTER THREE

The Story of Cygnus

Phaethon could not believe his eyes. He had traveled east to the Palace of the Sun. The building was beautiful. It glittered gold and bronze and shone with bright light. But Phaethon was nervous. He had come here to meet Apollo, the Sun god. Phaethon's mother, Clymene (KLIH-muh-nee), had said Apollo was his father. Phaethon had come to find out the truth. He stepped inside the glittering building.

Apollo greeted Phaethon warmly. He really was Phaethon's father. Phaethon was relieved. But he was not sure anyone would believe him. Apollo said he would grant any wish Phaethon had to prove his love for his son. Phaethon knew immediately what he wanted. He told his father he wished to drive the Sun chariot.

Clymene told Phaethon his father was the Sun god. Phaethon traveled to the Palace of the Sun for proof.

Phaethon begged Apollo to let him drive the Sun chariot.

Apollo knew this was a bad idea. At first, he said no. Driving the chariot was dangerous. Phaethon would have to avoid monsters that lived as constellations in the sky. Taurus the Bull, Leo the Lion, Cancer the Crab, and Scorpius the Scorpion would try to attack him. Plus, the Sun chariot's horses were strong and fast. They breathed fire. They needed a strong hand on the reins. Not even Zeus, the king of the gods, could control the horses. Apollo told his son that driving the chariot would be a punishment, not a reward. He told him to ask for something else.

But Phaethon begged. Apollo had promised! And if Phaethon drove the Sun chariot, his friends would know that Apollo really was his father. In the end, Apollo had no choice but to keep his promise. So he tried to give Phaethon advice. But Phaethon was so excited he hardly listened to his father. He stepped into the chariot. The gates opened, and the chariot took off!

Right away, the horses could tell they had a different driver. Phaethon was not as heavy as his father. Phaethon tried his best, but he could not control the horses. They ran all over the sky. The Sun came close to the Earth. Gaia (GY-uh), the goddess of the Earth, asked Zeus for help. The Sun chariot was out of control. Rivers and lakes were drying up, creating deserts. The Earth was burning. Its people were suffering.

There was only one thing to do. Zeus threw a lightning bolt. Phaethon was thrown from the chariot. The horses ran to their stable in the west. The Earth was safe again.

ZEUS THE SWAN

Other Greek myths say the Cygnus constellation represents Zeus. Zeus was the king of the gods. But he often fell in love with women on Earth. He would often disguise himself to romance these women. In two different stories, he turned himself into a swan on his quest for love.

Zeus knocked Phaethon out of the sky with a lightning bolt.

Phaethon's family and friends mourned his death. His seven sisters became poplar trees. Cygnus became a swan.

But Phaethon was not safe. He fell from the sky into a river. Phaethon's friend and relative Cygnus saw him fall. Cygnus was horrified. He had to save his friend! He dove into the water to rescue Phaethon. He plunged in again and again. But he was not able to save Phaethon. Cygnus began to cry. As he did, his cries changed. His neck became longer. His body was covered in feathers. Cygnus had transformed into a swan. The gods were touched by Cygnus's act of friendship. They placed him into the sky. The swan constellation is Cygnus. The Milky Way is the river. The swan continues to dive as the stars rise and set.

This constellation reminds people of Cygnus's friendship. But the story of Phaethon is also a warning. Phaethon really believed that he could drive the Sun chariot. His **arrogance** got him into trouble.

CHAPTER FOUR

The Myth of Cygnus in Other Cultures

People from societies all over the world recognized Cygnus. Some, like the Greeks, saw a bird. The Cree people of North America also see Cygnus as a long-necked bird. Their constellation is called *Niska*, the Goose. The Ojibwe call it *Ajijaak*, the **Crane**.

A story from China describes the constellation as a bridge made of birds. Zhi Nü (SHEE-noo), the Weaving Girl, wove beautiful robes from the clouds. One day, Zhi Nü and her sisters went to Earth. Niu Lang (nee-yoo-LONG), a **cowherd**, saw the sisters. He fell in love with Zhi Nü. Soon, Zhi Nü and Niu Lang were married. They had two sons. They lived on Earth for several years. They loved each other and were very happy.

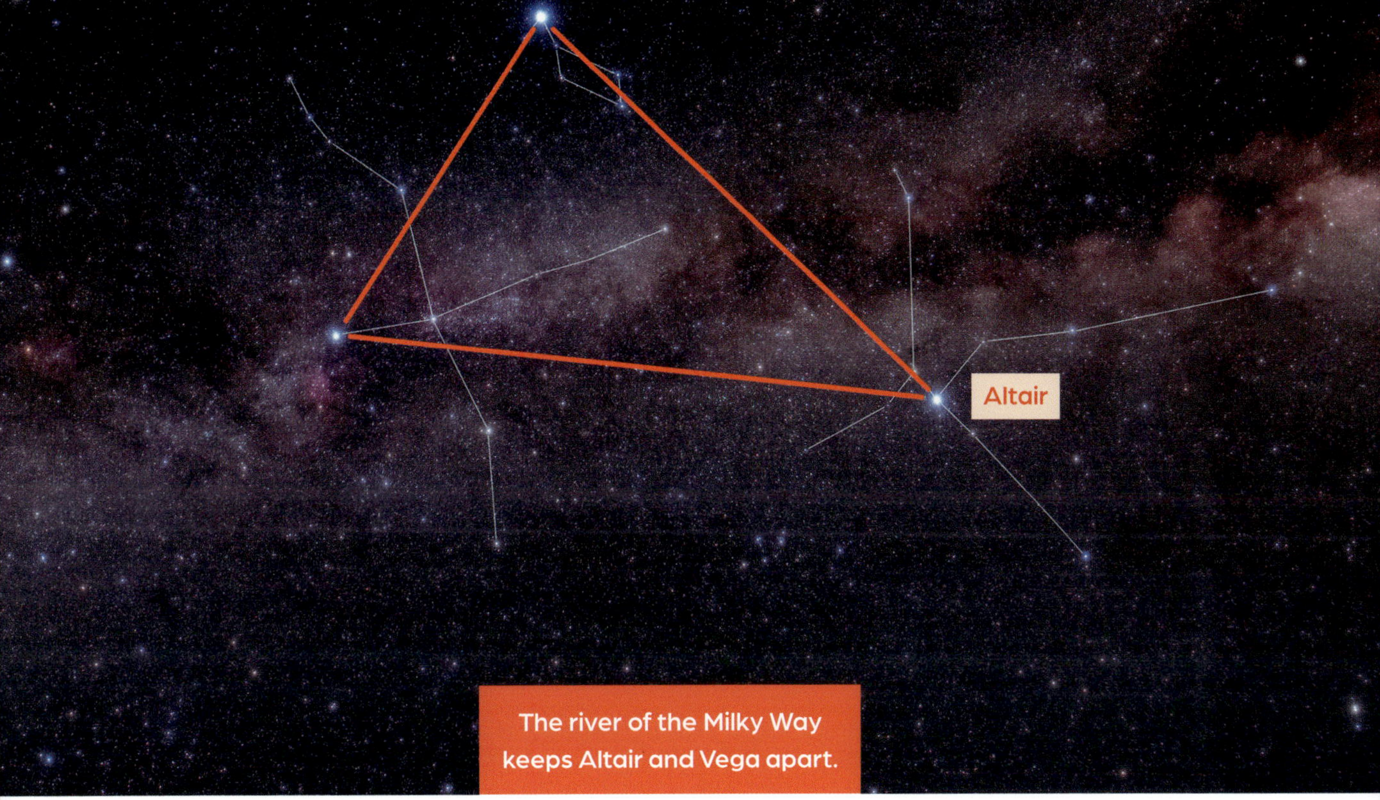

The river of the Milky Way keeps Altair and Vega apart.

But Zhi Nü's mother called her back to the sky. She was angry that Zhi Nü was not doing her job. Zhi Nü was sad to be back in the sky. She missed her family. And Niu Lang and his sons missed Zhi Nü. They wondered if they would ever be happy again.

But Niu Lang's bull had magical powers. He told Niu Lang how to find his wife. Niu Lang flew into the sky with his sons. Zhi Nü raced to meet her family. But before they could reach each other, the Queen Mother drew her hairpin across the sky. It sliced the sky, creating a river between Zhi Nü and Niu Lang.

The Qixi Festival is known as Tanabata in Japan and Chilseok in Korea.

Everyone felt sorry for the couple. So every year, on the seventh day of the seventh month, all the magpies in the world fly into the sky. These black-and-white birds are related to crows. They make a bridge for Zhi Nü and Niu Lang to visit each other. The magpie bridge is the constellation of Cygnus. Zhi Nü is Vega, and Lyra is her weaving loom. Niu Lang and his sons are the three brightest stars in Aquila, with Niu Lang as Altair. The Qixi (CHEE-shee) Festival happens on the seventh day of the seventh month. This is when Vega and Altair are closest. The festival is sometimes called Chinese Valentine's Day.

Other stories do not say Cygnus is a bird. These include other Native American stories. The Shoshone of Wyoming, Idaho, Nevada, and Utah see Cygnus as part of a grizzly bear racing up a snowy mountain. When he ran, the snow that he kicked up became the Milky Way. The Zuni of New Mexico see the Summer Triangle as the heart of a huge constellation called the Chief of the Sky. The Chumash of southern California see Cygnus as part of the Scorpion Woman. She guards the road to the Land of the Dead, which is the Milky Way. Souls have to pass by Scorpion Woman to cross a bridge. Only good souls can cross over.

MAUI'S FISHHOOK

To native Hawaiians, the Summer Triangle is a coil of fishing line. It is attached to Maui's fishhook, or Scorpius. Maui is a hero from Polynesian stories. In one story, Maui uses his fishhook to pull islands up out of the ocean. In the summer and fall, sailors use these stars to find their way on the ocean.

CHAPTER FIVE

How to Find Cygnus in the Sky

In the Northern **Hemisphere**, Cygnus is visible in the summer. To find it, look east. Find the three stars of the Summer Triangle. These are Vega, Altair, and Deneb. Deneb is the left corner of the triangle. Vega is on the top. Altair is the lowest of the three stars.

Cygnus looks like a cross, with Deneb at the top. The bottom of the cross is Albireo. Albireo is between Vega and Altair.

In places without much **light pollution**, people can see the stripe of the Milky Way in the sky. Cygnus flies along the Milky Way from north to south. In the Northern Hemisphere, Cygnus is high overhead from July to September.

In the Southern Hemisphere, Cygnus is low in the northern sky. It is visible in July and August. This is winter in the Southern Hemisphere.

The Summer Triangle helps viewers find Cygnus.

GLOSSARY

ancient (AYN-shunt) Something that is ancient is very old or belongs to times long ago. Ancient Greeks told the story of Phaethon and Cygnus.

arrogance (AYR-uh-genss) Arrogance is when a person thinks they are better than other people. Phaethon's arrogance cost him his life.

astronomers (uh-STRAW-nuh-murz) Astronomers are scientists who study stars and other objects in space. Astronomers throughout history have recognized Cygnus.

chariot (CHAYR-ee-uht) A chariot is a small vehicle pulled by horses. Apollo pulled the sun across the sky in a chariot.

cowherd (KOW-hurd) A cowherd is a person who takes care of cows. Niu Lang was a cowherd.

crane (KRAYN) A crane is a large bird with a long neck. Ojibwe storytellers see Cygnus as a crane.

galaxy (GAL-uhk-see) A galaxy is a group of dust, gases, and billions of stars held together by gravity. Earth is in the Milky Way galaxy.

hemisphere (HEH-mih-sfeer) A hemisphere is half of a sphere. Earth is divided into the Northern Hemisphere and Southern Hemisphere.

light pollution (LYT poll-OO-shun) Light pollution is a glow in the sky caused by streetlights and house lights. Light pollution can make it hard to see stars.

light-years (LYT-yeerz) Light-years are used to measure very large distances in space. One light-year equals the distance that light travels in one year (about 6 trillion miles, or 9 trillion km). The nearest star to the Sun is 4 light-years away.

orbiting (OR-bih-ting) When an object is orbiting another object, it takes a rounded path around it. The Kepler spacecraft discovered planets orbiting stars in Pegasus.

X-rays (EX-rayz) X-rays are light rays that carry more energy than the light that humans can see. The gas around a black hole produces X-rays.

FAST FACTS

- Constellations are groupings of stars in the sky that form pictures. Stars are glowing balls of gas throughout the universe. The Sun is a star.
- Cygnus is a constellation that looks like a swan. Cygnus contains two asterisms. These are the Northern Cross and the Summer Triangle.
- Societies around the world had their own constellations and stories about them.
- The most common story about Cygnus comes from the Greeks. Cygnus was a friend and relative of Phaethon, the son of Apollo. Phaethon died after trying to drive Apollo's Sun chariot. Cygnus cried for his friend and turned into a swan.
- In the Chinese story of Cygnus, the stars are a bridge of magpies. Once a year, the bridge reunites a husband and wife separated by the Milky Way.
- Cree storytellers see Cygnus as a goose. In Ojibwe tradition, Cygnus is a crane. Other cultures see fishing line, a grizzly bear, a great Chief, or the Scorpion Woman in Cygnus's stars.
- Cygnus is bright and easy to find in the sky.

ONE STRIDE FURTHER

- What does the constellation of Cygnus look like to you?
- Which story about Cygnus do you like best? Why?
- Do you think that Apollo should have allowed Phaethon to drive the Sun chariot? Why or why not?
- The stories of the constellations are very old. Why do you think we still tell them today?

FIND OUT MORE

IN THE LIBRARY

Beall, Abigail. *An Anthology of Stargazing: A Collection of Stars and Constellations*. New York, NY: DK Publishing, 2025.

Perdew, Laura. *Investigating Light Pollution*. Parker, CO: The Child's World, 2023.

Sheldon-Dean, Hannah. *Who's Who? Greek Mythology*. Nashville, TN: Applesauce Press, 2024.

ON THE WEB

Visit our website for links about Cygnus:

childsworld.com/links

Note to Parents, Caregivers, Teachers, and Librarians: We routinely verify our web links to make sure they are safe and active sites. So encourage your readers to check them out!

INDEX